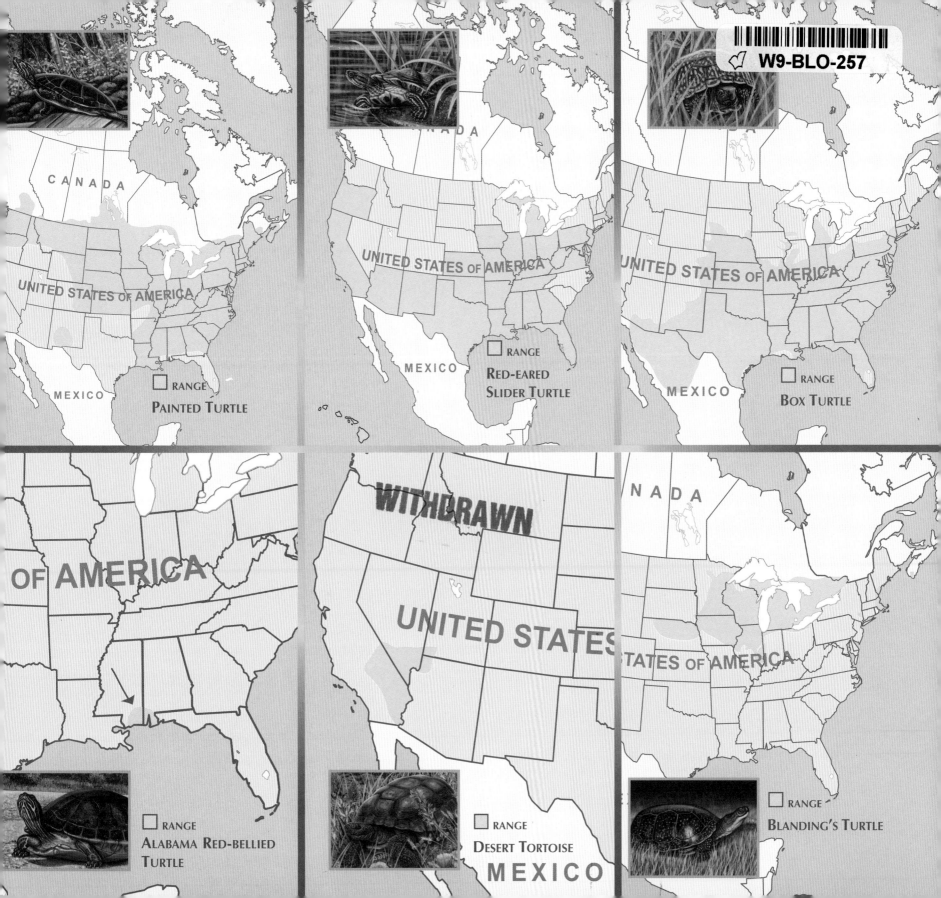

□ RANGE
PAINTED TURTLE

□ RANGE
RED-EARED
SLIDER TURTLE

□ RANGE
BOX TURTLE

□ RANGE
ALABAMA RED-BELLIED
TURTLE

□ RANGE
DESERT TORTOISE

□ RANGE
BLANDING'S TURTLE

WITHDRAWN

A PLACE FOR
TURTLES

For Gerard

—M. S.

For my precious turtledove,
Annabella Patrycja Bond

—H. B.

Published by
PEACHTREE PUBLISHERS
1700 Chattahoochee Avenue
Atlanta, Georgia 30318-2112

www.peachtree-online.com

Book design by Loraine M. Joyner
Composition by Maureen Withee
Illustrations created in acrylic on cold press illustration board.
Title typeset in Hardlyworthit; main text typeset in Monotype's Century
Schoolbook with Optima initial capitals. Sidebars typeset in Optima.

Printed and manufactured in Malaysia
10 9 8 7 6 5 4 3 2 1
First Edition

ISBN 13: 978-1-56145-693-2
ISBN 10: 1-56145-693-4

Cataloguing-in-Publication data for this title is available through the
Library of Congress.

A PLACE FOR
TURTLES

Written by
Melissa Stewart

Illustrated by
Higgins Bond

PEACHTREE
ATLANTA

Turtles make our world a better place. But sometimes people do things that make it hard for them to live and grow.

If we work together to help these special creatures, there will always be a place for turtles.

A LOOK AT TURTLES

Turtles are closely related to snakes, lizards, and crocodiles. They all belong to a group of animals called reptiles. Some turtles spend most of their lives on land. Other turtles live in lakes, rivers, or the ocean. But all turtles hatch from tough leathery eggs laid on land. Newly hatched turtles are tiny. Except for their size, they look just like their parents.

spotted turtle

Like all living things, turtles need safe places to raise their young. Some turtles have trouble building nests when new kinds of plants spread into their home habitat.

When people find ways to control the new plants, turtles can live and grow.

BOG TURTLE

Because purple loosestrife has pretty purple flowers and can be used as a medicine, European settlers brought it to North America. But when thick clusters of loosestrife began growing in wetlands, bog turtles couldn't find sunny spots for their nests. In 1997, people started using beetles to control the loosestrife. Now bog turtles have many more good places to build their nests.

Young turtles don't stand a chance when people add fish to lakes and ponds.

WESTERN POND TURTLE

As Americans moved west in the 1800s, they added largemouth bass to the lakes and ponds near their new homes. These new fish needed lots of food, and tiny turtle hatchlings made a good meal. By 1990, there were only 150 western pond turtles left in the entire state of Washington. When people noticed the problem, they began collecting the hatchlings and taking them to nearby zoos. Zoo employees cared for the young turtles until they were large enough to survive on their own in their native habitat. Today more than a thousand western pond turtles live in Washington.

When people collect newly hatched turtles and raise them in safe places, turtles can live and grow.

Adult turtles face many dangers too. A sea turtle can die if it gets trapped in a fishing net.

When fishing crews use nets that have special escape hatches, turtles can live and grow.

LOGGERHEAD TURTLE

In the past, hundreds of thousands of loggerhead turtles died each year in fishing nets used to catch shrimp. But in 1988, the U.S. Congress passed a law that requires fishing nets to have a turtle excluder device—a sort of trapdoor that turtles can use but shrimp can't. Since that law was passed, the number of net-related turtle deaths has decreased nearly 70 percent.

Because plastic shopping bags look like jellyfish, sea turtles sometimes eat them by mistake. The plastic can clog the turtle's stomach, causing it to starve to death.

LEATHERBACK TURTLE

In the mid-1980s, stores across North America switched from paper shopping bags to plastic ones. Because plastic never breaks down, over time millions of shopping bags ended up in the ocean where they could harm leatherback turtles. Today many families bring their own reusable cloth bags to the grocery store. Small changes like this can help save sea turtles.

When people stop using plastic shopping bags, turtles can live and grow.

Some turtles taste so delicious that people eat too many of them.

When lawmakers stop people from hunting the tasty reptiles, turtles can live and grow.

DIAMONDBACK TERRAPIN

In the late 1800s, turtle soup was so popular that people in Maryland and Virginia caught close to 100,000 diamondback terrapins every year. By the 1920s, there were almost none of these turtles left. Many restaurants stopped serving turtle soup, but some people continued to eat terrapins. Today, it is illegal to hunt diamondback terrapins in nine states, and the turtles are struggling to survive.

Many people let their dogs run free when they go hiking in natural areas. But curious dogs can injure turtles and other small animals.

PAINTED TURTLE

When pet owners go to forests, wetlands, and other wild places, they like to let their dogs run free. But dogs are hunters. Their natural instincts tell them to chase and attack smaller animals. Keeping dogs on a leash can save the lives of turtles and other wild creatures.

When hikers keep their dogs on leashes, turtles can live and grow.

S ome turtles have such colorful bodies and shells that people like to keep them as pets.

RED-EARED SLIDER TURTLE

Because red-eared slider turtles have colorful bodies and shells with interesting patterns, many people are tempted to take them home. But a turtle is a wild animal. It can't form a special bond with people, and living in a terrarium is stressful. It is against the law to catch or sell young turtles, but it's best to let all turtles—even the older ones—live in their natural habitats.

When people stop collecting these beautiful reptiles,
turtles can live and grow.

Many people think it's fun to watch turtle races at fairs, picnics, and rodeos. But when turtles from different places come into contact with one another, they can get sick.

When people learn the truth about these races, turtles can live and grow.

BOX TURTLE

Each year, people catch 15,000 to 25,000 box turtles and enter them in local races. During each race, turtles from different locations may pass germs to one another. Many turtles get sick and die after a race. Even if the turtles stay healthy, they will have trouble surviving if they are not returned to the exact same spot where they were found. Racing turtles may seem like fun, but turtles are better off when people leave them alone.

Turtles have dark bodies, and they move slowly. People driving cars near turtle habitats may not see them—until it's too late.

ALABAMA RED-BELLIED TURTLE

Even though people have been working to save Alabama red-bellied turtles for many years, these animals still face many dangers. Between 2001 and 2006, more than 400 Alabama red-bellied turtles were killed trying to cross a four-lane highway called Mobile Causeway. In 2007, workers built a 4.3-mile-long fence along the highway, so turtles couldn't wander onto the road.

Alabama red-bellied turtle

When people build turtle-proof fences along busy highways,
turtles can live and grow.

Turtles have trouble surviving when their natural homes are destroyed. Some turtles can only live in sandy desert areas with plenty of low shrubs.

When people protect these natural places,
turtles can live and grow.

DESERT TORTOISE

In the 1950s, Las Vegas, Nevada, became a popular place to live. As the city grew, workers built homes, businesses, and parking lots on the land where desert tortoises lived. Soon the turtles were in trouble. In 1989, the United States Fish and Wildlife Service added desert tortoises to the endangered species list. Now people are working hard to protect the desert areas where the turtles live.

O ther turtles can only survive in shallow marshes and ponds.

BLANDING'S TURTLE

In 1996, LaGrange, New York, needed to make their high school larger. But the only place to expand was a wetland where Blanding's turtles lived. To solve the problem, workers carefully moved soil and plants to a nearby location and created another wetland for the turtles. Now students keep a close watch on the Blanding's turtles and their habitat. So far, the turtles seem to like their new home.

Blanding's turtle

When people create new wetlands, turtles can live and grow.

When too many turtles die, other living things may also have trouble surviving.

That's why it's so important to protect turtles and the places where they live.

OTHER ANIMALS NEED TURTLES

Turtles are an important part of animal food chains. Turtle eggs are good sources of food for snakes, lizards, otters, raccoons, badgers, rats, herons, and gulls. Adult turtles are eaten by coyotes, foxes, weasels, minks, skunks, opossums, eagles, osprey, alligators, crocodiles, and sharks. Without a thriving population of turtles, many other creatures would go hungry.

Turtles have lived on Earth for more than 220 million years.

Sometimes people do things that can harm turtles. But there are many ways you can help these special creatures live far into the future.

HELPING TURTLES

❖ Do not catch and keep turtles. Let them live in their natural environment.

❖ Do not buy turtles at a pet store. Turtles are wild animals and should live in their natural homes.

❖ If someone gives you a turtle, do not release it in a wild place. It could make other turtles sick.

❖ Do not throw trash into any body of water.

❖ Do not pour household cleaners or other chemicals down the drain.

❖ Join a group of people working to protect or restore rivers, lakes, streams, ponds, or ocean areas near your home.

TERRIFIC TURTLE TIDBITS

No one knows exactly how many kinds of turtles live on Earth. So far, scientists have discovered more than 250 different species. About fifty kinds of turtles live in North America.

The bog turtle is the smallest turtle on Earth. It is just 4 inches long. The leatherback turtle is the world's largest turtle. It can grow more than 6 feet long and weigh as much as an elephant.

bog turtle

You can usually tell whether a turtle spends most of its time in the water or on land just by looking at it. Most land turtles, like box turtles and desert tortoises, have high, domed shells. Turtles that live in rivers, lakes, or the ocean have low, flat shells.

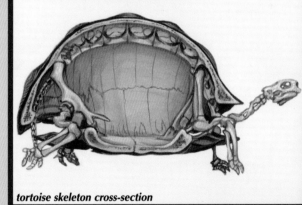
tortoise skeleton cross-section

A turtle's shell is made up of sixty different bones.

Most turtles that live in cold places hibernate during the winter, but people have seen Blanding's turtles swimming under the ice.

Galapagos tortoise

A **turtle** spends most of its life in the water. Most turtles have webbed feet that help them swim. A **tortoise** spends its whole life on land. Tortoises have rounded, stumpy feet that are perfect for walking. A **terrapin** spends time on land and in the water. Terrapins usually live in swampy areas.

Some turtles can live more than 100 years. A few species can survive more than a year without food.

Acknowledgments

The author wishes to thank Andrea Beshara, a turtle research biologist who serves as a naturalist instructor and education animal coordinator at the Oklahoma City Zoo in Oklahoma City, Oklahoma, for her help in preparing this manuscript.

Selected Bibliography

BOOKS AND ARTICLES

Berger, Melvin. *Look Out for Turtles!* New York: Harper Collins, 1996.*

Chiang, Mona. "The Plight of the Turtle." *Science World.* May 9, 2003, pp. 8–14.*

Davies, Nicola. *One Tiny Turtle.* Cambridge, MA: Candlewick, 2005.*

"Don' t Take the Turtles." *Boy's Quest.* April-May 2003, pp. 20–21.*

Ernst, Carl and Jeffrey Lovich. *Turtles of the United States and Canada.* Baltimore, MD: Johns Hopkins University Press, 2009.

Mlot, Christine. "FWS Proposes Protection for Bog Turtle." *Science News.* February 8, 1997, p. 92.

Sayre, April Pulley. *Turtle, Turtle, Watch Out!* Watertown, MA: Charlesbridge, 2010.*

Rainer, David. "Alabama Red-Bellied Turtle Gets Added Protection." *Outdoor Alabama.* http://dcnr.state.al.us/oaonline/RBturtle08.cfm

Winner, Cherie. *Everything Reptile: What Kids Really Want to Know About Reptiles.* Minnetonka, MN: NorthWord Books for Young Readers, 2004.*

WEBSITES

"Blanding's Turtle: Habitat Restoration Project." Hudsonia: A Non-profit Environmental Reasearch Group. URL at http://hudsonia.org/programs/conservation-ecology/blandings-turtle/

"Saving Blanding's Turtles." TeacherTube video created by students at Arlington High School, LaGrange, NY. URL at http://www.teachertube.com/viewVideo.php?video_id=167497&title=Blandings_Turtle *

*Recommended resources for young explorers

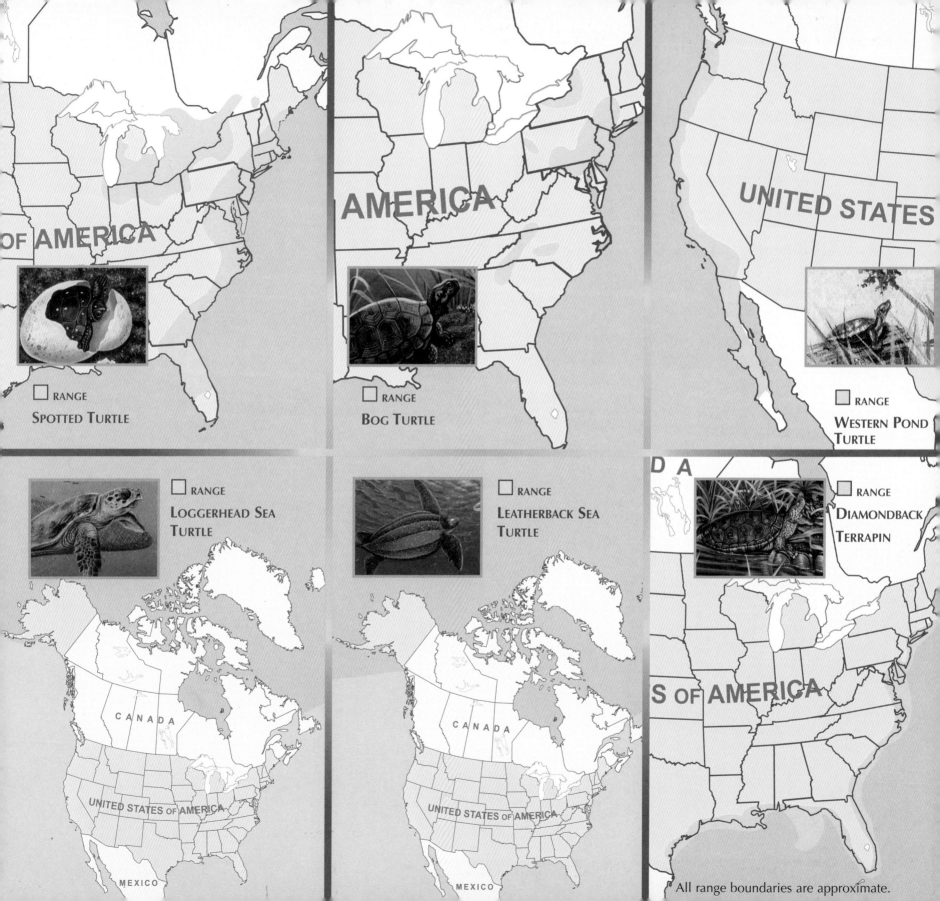

☐ RANGE
SPOTTED TURTLE

☐ RANGE
BOG TURTLE

☐ RANGE
WESTERN POND TURTLE

☐ RANGE
LOGGERHEAD SEA TURTLE

☐ RANGE
LEATHERBACK SEA TURTLE

☐ RANGE
DIAMONDBACK TERRAPIN

CANADA

UNITED STATES OF AMERICA

MEXICO

CANADA

UNITED STATES OF AMERICA

MEXICO

D A

S OF AMERICA

All range boundaries are approximate.